The Azusa Street Revival:

WRAPPED IN SWADDLING CLOTHES LYING IN A MANGER

PROPHET ELIJAH HILL

Copyright June 2006 by Elijah Hill All rights reserved.

Scripture quotations are taken from the **Holy Bible,**
KING JAMES VERSION AND TODAY'S INTERNATIONAL
VERSION, Copyright 2002 & 2004 by the International Bible
Society. Used by permission of Zondervan. All rights reserved.

Cover design by Anwar Gay
www.swamp_graphics@yahoo.com

All rights reserved. No part of this book may be reproduced or utilized in any form or by any means, electronic, mechanical, including photocopying, recording or by any informational storage and retrieval system, without permission.

Published by
International Soaring Eagles' Press
www.internationalsoaringeaglesministeries.org
preachingmama@hotmail.com
Selfridge, Michigan

Inquiries should be addressed to:
www.prophetelijahhill.com
cogic@prophetelijahhill.com
Elijah Hill, Th.B, MBA
214-636-7668

Table of Contents

Dedication

Chapter 1 A Son Was Born	5
Chapter 2 No Room in the Inn	29
Chapter 3 Lying in a Manger	41
Chapter 4 No Divisions Among You	68
Chapter 5 Contending for the faith	84
Chapter 6 Conclusion	116

Dedication

This book is dedicated ...

To my Father Ernest Eugene Hill who has been a great inspiration to me, and one of my greatest fans. He always has words of encouragement to say to cause me to identify with my own inner strength.

To two angels that God brought into my life, Missionary Diane Kiel and Pastor P.K. Roberts. Without your assistance and prayers this project would never have been completed.

Finally, I thank God for choosing me to share with the Body of Christ this precious historical information. If we don't know our history – our future will suffer for the lack of strategic planning.

Chapter 1

And she brought forth her first-born Son! St. Luke 2:7

In the words of Pastor William J. Seymour published in his November 1906 newspaper he describes the beginning of his work, it reads:

"In the vicinity of a tombstone shop, stables and lumber yard (a fortunate vicinity because no one complains of all-night meetings) you find a two-story, white-washed old building. You hardly expect heavenly visitations there, unless you remember the stable at Bethlehem. "[9]

"It is noticeable how free all nationalities feel. If a Mexican or German cannot speak English, he gets up

*and speaks in his own tongue and feels quite at home for the Spirit interprets through the face and people say amen. No instrument that God can use is rejected on account of color or dress or lack of education. This is why God has built up the work."*9

This book is written to give a better understanding of several events that occurred surrounding the "outpouring" of the Holy Spirit within the Twentieth Century Pentecostal Movement in America in and around 1906 in Los Angeles, California. Over the course of time there has been many misunderstanding surrounding who did what, and what was the strategic methodology that God implemented to birth-out this Pentecostal Movement in America in 1906.

One of the questions historically that comes to mind is, who is the father or founder of this movement, Charles F. Parham or William J. Seymour. First of all, we must understand that we are looking back on events that are now edged in stone, and cannot be changed.

Nevertheless, God finally orchestrated and directed the outcome of these events.

Charles F. Parham started the classical Pentecostal theology in Topeka, Kansas in 1901. This occurred five years prior to the Los Angeles event called the Azusa Street Revival. There had always been scattered instances of individuals experiencing the infilling of the Holy Ghost. In 1901, Parham established a school, where the student body began to not just learn, but received the First Century New Testament Pentecostal experience.

This was the first organized educational format that began to impact several surrounding Midwestern states in America. In December 1905, Parham moved his Bible School to Houston, Texas. This was strategically important in history, because this is where William J. Seymour learns from Parham's school about the theology of "initial evidence" of receiving the Holy Spirit and speaking in tongues.

In 1903, Seymour moved to Houston, Texas and ended up pastoring Lucy Farrow's church. She later introduces Seymour to Parham's Bible school teaching of Pentecost.

Charles F. Parham

The end result is Seymour accepts Parham's teaching after sitting outside a window listening in because of Parham's segregated practices there in Houston.

"In 1905 Seymour moved to Houston, Texas, in search of his family. Here he began to attend a Holiness church pastored by Lucy Farrow. When Pastor Farrow went to Kansas in 1905 to work as governess in the home of Charles Fox Parham (1873-1929), a holiness preacher who had been leading a Pentecostal movement in the Midwest since 1901? Seymour was asked to become pastor of the church." (Mcgee Page 780)[24]

At this time in American society Jim Crow was at its height in America. Now, Charles F. Parham the founder of the school of Modern Day Pentecostal theology believed in racism, and practiced it as the majority of citizen in America did. Therefore, when Seymour came to him about attending his classes he was refused to participate because he could not sit in the same classes as the white students.

Bishop William J. Seymour

William J. Seymour was born in 1870, and he was the son of ex-slaves. He understood that this Jim Crow policy of Parham was normalcy for his life. Yet, he wanted this greater knowledge and understanding of the bible, therefore an arrangement was made for him to sit in a hallway outside of Parham's classes, in order for him to learn about glossolalia as a present day sign of the Holy Spirit Baptism.

Charles Parham's ministry was specifically for white Americans. The reason why I infer this is because his ministry style was teaching in an educational environment, and according to Jim Crow laws he abided by and believed scriptural that this was God's will.

This chapter title is, "She brought forth her first born son." My purpose is not to just tell the history of the evolution of modern day Pentecost, but to demonstrate God's strategies and reasons for setting a stage that will propel the movement.

In the evolution of Pentecost first of all if you take Lucy Farrow out of the equation William Seymour would have never been positioned in place to become the dynamic spiritual leader God had chosen him to be. Lucy Farrow is pastoring a church in Houston, Texas, and this just so happens to be the strategic church that God leads William Seymour to join while living in the Houston area in 1903.

Farrow being the pastor, as God would have it develops a solid ministerial relationship with Seymour over the next two years. This relationship would become very important because later she is offered a position to serve as governess of Charles Parham's school in Topeka, Kansas.

Historically, during this era in 1905 Ms. Farrow basically was hired as a servant to do what most black women did for white people in height of the Jim Crow in America. They took care of the needs white person's household like: cooking their food, cleaning their house, washing their clothes, and raising their children in the place of their mothers.

In most cases they had to come in through the back door, and maintain the utmost of respect for these white individuals while serving in their homes. They lived as slaves or servants because of the laws of segregation and Jim Crow in American society.

Yet, God places this woman within Parham's segregated white community. He allows her to get close enough to his teaching to indirectly learn about the teaching of (glossolalia) as the initial evidence of speaking in tongues.

In American society, the way segregation separated the white and black races with violence as the end result if an African American violated one of these ordinances inside a white individual's home or openly in their community. Nevertheless, Ms. Farrow while doing her daily duties within Parham's home and school was blessed to over hear his teachings. As a result of her working in this environment she desired the Holy Spirit infilling for herself.

Obviously, she investigated these New Testament scriptures for herself in the quietness and lateness of the night, or early in the morning after prayer before rising up to go to work. Her ministerial background as a pastor herself afforded her many opportunities to search for deeper understandings of God's word.

I am reminded of Ms. Farrow spiritually as an Esther in the Bible who was given access to the palace to become governess of Parham's house and school. Yet, God had strategically placed her there for the purpose of bringing a message of deliverance and greater spiritual liberty towards her people (Esther 4:8).

History records that it was Lucy Farrow that was the first African American to receive the experience of speaking in tongues, while being a hired servant in Parham's religious community. She really was not hired to learn about the Baptism of the Holy Ghost, but she, being a minister of the gospel, took the time after hours to seek God to experience this next level of intimacy with Him.

There are times that God gives us access to things in order for us to be a blessing to others because where God has placed us it is not just about us. In the Bible, Esther was put in a place where others could not go. Similarly, Ms. Farrow during Jim Crow being an African American woman who was allowed the liberty as Parham's hired servant to get close enough to learn of this New Testament promise for Modern Day Pentecost went where others were not allowed.

Charles Parham personally did not believe in African Americans worshipping with whites, therefore her experiencing the Baptism of the Holy Ghost was not something Parham would have been a part of because of his segregated views. Nevertheless, to Parham's surprise Lucy Farrow starts speaking in tongues and worshipping

God in a more expressive way like most African Americans do.

If you will notice that in the New Testament when the Holy Spirit began to pour out his Spirit for the first time, it states Acts 10:45, 46, it states:

45. And they of the circumcision, which believed, were astonished, as many as came with Peter, because that on the Gentiles also was poured out the gift of the Holy Ghost. 46. For they heard them speak with tongues, and magnify God.

The Jews for the first time witnessed racial and ethnic barriers washed away by Pentecost falling on a segregated group of people the Gentiles. This was unheard of before this time just as it was unheard of when Charles Parham saw that Lucy Farrow had received the baptism of the Holy Ghost.

Parham being a person, who abided by Jim Crow laws, did not want it told that a black was experiencing this type of worship experience. I am sure he tried to control her experience reminding her of the main purpose he had brought her to his religious community to take care of the big house.

When an individual first receives the Holy Spirit Baptism it is very difficult to hold back, since it is the first time God allows this type of rivers of living water to flow out of your being. It has a supernatural force, and like a rushing might, wind.

Therefore, Lucy Farrow was left with a choice, to be happy about her new job, which had given her access to the big house, or continue her spiritual experience. My belief is that sometimes God places women in strategic positions, and allows them to have access to something that African American men cannot enjoy fully as their sisters. These sisters have been brought to the kingdom for such a time as this to assist their brothers and sisters.

It could have been easy for Ms. Farrow to be content with this great servant position, and not think about her people other African Americans who were at this time, being disfranchised of this glorious New Testament teaching and experience. The door was now opened in the Spirit of God through Ms. Farrow's experience to begin the seeds of Modern Day Pentecost flooding into the black community. This demonstration of God's outpouring of the Spirit shows that religious and political segregation would have a challenge to contain the infilling of the Holy Spirit across racial and ethnic lines.

As history records, Lucy Farrow chose to go with her supernatural experience. She did not allow the present rules of society or the benefit of dwelling in a prestigious place to be her tradeoff. Rather, she fulfilled her divine destiny by going and tells others what God had done. The scripture states in Esther 4:8, that:

8. Also he gave him the copy of the writing of the decree that was given at Shushan to destroy them, to shew it unto Esther, and to declare it unto her, and to charge her that she should go in unto the king, to make supplication unto him, and to make request before him for her people.

    Sometimes the place that God sends you has been preordained so that you can share it with others. Mordecai told Esther that just because you are in the king's house do not forget about the others on the outside of the place that you have been blessed to go into. If you do not submit to God then your people's deliverance will arise from another place, but you will have disobeyed God (Esther 4:16).

    Lucy Farrow decides to leave Parham's Bethel Bible College and religious community as his hired servant to become a very significant instrument in bringing forth one of the most notable African American males into position for divine destiny. This black man, William J. Seymour, would become one of the most important figures in the Modern Day Pentecostal Movement.

She left Topeka, Kansas and returned to Houston, Texas in October of 1906 to spread the news that Pentecost had come for African Americans, and that it was a present day experience that she had experienced for herself. She shares this information with Pastor William Seymour, who is presently pastoring her church.

Parham realizes that what has happened is the move of God, and if he was to remain the father of this movement he needed to be connected in some area of the country that shared his same beliefs. Charles Parham up roots his whole school, and comes to Houston, where Lucy Farrow is to establish his Bible school ministry in that area.

Ironically, Lucy Farrow is the vessel God uses that divinely connects Parham to Seymour. She obviously influences Parham to make arrangements to allow the present pastor of her former church, Pastor Seymour, to sit outside of Parham's classes.

Parham refuses to have a black man sitting in his classroom with the rest of the whites. Ms. Farrow, obviously because of her past position, has developed a close relationship to Parham where she can say things to him that would have not been allowed in a normal Jim Crow environment.

She continues to argue the point that he should allow God to have his way, and that if he poured out his Spirit on her then he needs an African American to share it with their community. Having an African American minister to share the New Testament revelation with other blacks suited Parham just fine as long as whites and blacks did not worship together. Therefore, he agreed to allow Seymour to sit not in the classroom with the whites, but outside in the hallway to overhear the doctrine Parham taught on the baptism of the Holy Ghost.

Lucy Farrow obviously has developed a relationship with both men, and is instrumental in God's plan to bring them together for a greater purpose. If we remove Lucy Farrow from the connection of Parham to Seymour what God had in mind for Azusa might not have taken place.

It is obvious that William Seymour in a Jim Crow environment could not have had this conversation with Parham. Surrounding himself learning with whites, or he could have been lynched being a black man requesting something that was against the laws of the in the Deep South.

The black man had to keep a low profile if any white individual observed him speaking with to much confidence to a white man. The cultural rules of America's white society dictated that a black man couldn't raised his voice, had to bow his head while speaking, and say, yes sir, to most white men in the Deep South. Expressing themselves any other way publicly was considered an insult and threat to white male's manhood, and this violation could possibly result in a black man being beaten or lynched for violating the segregated rules of the south.

This is the reason God selected Lucy Farrow who helped to birth out her first born spiritual son for Modern day Pentecost, William J. Seymour. Obviously, God had shown her something about his destiny that even Seymour probably did not understand.

Ms. Farrow, two years later would find herself positioned right along side Seymour at the Azusa Street Mission laying hands on many future leaders of the Modern Day Pentecostal movement. She was known to have the gift like Peter did in the book of Acts, where they would send for Peter and John, and when they would lay hands on them they would receive the baptism of the Holy Ghost with the evidence of speaking in tongues.

Here is a quote from William Seymour's publication describing her impact on the Azusa Street Revival. It states in September 1906,

"Ms. Lucy F. Farrow, God's anointed handmaid, who came some four months ago from Houston, Texas, to

Los Angeles, bring the full Gospel, and whom God has greatly used as she laid her hands on many who have received the Pentecost and the gift of tongues, has now returned to Houston, enroute to Norfolk, Virginia. This is her old home, which she left as a girl, being sold into slavery in the south. The Lord, she feels, is now calling her back. Sister Farrow, Bro. W.J. Seymour and Bro. J. A. Warren were the three that the Lord sent from Houston as messengers of the full gospel."[9]

Ms. Farrow was concerned for her own people, and she could not for get that it was her heritage to reach back for her own. By biological birth she was the niece of the famous Abolitionist Fredrick Douglas, who remembered his own people despite God allowing him to become an advisor to one of American's Presidents (Abraham Lincoln) during the Emancipation Proclamations in America's history.

Therefore, Farrows' position was for Charles Parham to obey God, and fulfill his divine destiny by training an African American minister to separately teach the black community about Modern Day Pentecost.

William Seymour's ministry would have not reached the heights that it had without this chosen handmaiden. He realized the necessity that a black male preacher needed in the assistance of his sister who had greater access to things when he was limited based on society's racial barriers.

William J. Seymour's spiritual midwife was Lucy Farrow the first to receive the baptism of the Holy Ghost as an African American in October 1905. He was therefore the first-born son that God allowed her to bring forth, who would become a catalyst to globalize Pentecostalism.

Often times God places a woman in a key strategic position to implement and fulfill his will on earth. The mother of Moses was a woman of strategy and determination who would not accept that her son had to die. If she had not devised a way to save the life of her son, there would be no great man called Moses.

Without Hannah, the mother of Samuel the Prophet, being the praying woman she was, Samuel would never had been born to anoint King David. Without Mary being an available and chaste vessel for God's use, Jesus would not have been able to pass through eternity with a prepared body, and fulfill what the prophets said, "A virgin shall conceive and bare a son....."

The ministerial relationship between Farrow and Seymour established a platform for Seymour having a great respect for women in ministry because he knew their significant role in building God's Kingdom. Later on at the Azusa Street Mission Seymour, would allow Farrow and other Azusa Street sisters to assist him in bringing many into the evidence of glossolalia. This relationship influenced the gender issues at the Azusa Street Revival, and many women served in leadership positions at Seymour's Church.

Chapter 2

There is no room in the Inn- St. Luke 2:7b

The beginning of this chapter is called, "There is no room in the Inn". The essence of what God had in mind during the Pentecostal Movement was for it to belong to all people. It was to reach out to every nation, ethnic group, and gender. Charles Parham's prejudice views would not allow God the flexibility to accomplish this purpose.

Parham would not have allowed blacks to experience Pentecost under an interracial worship experience because he believed in Jim Crow and segregationist practices. There was no room in the end within Parham's heart to understand the magnitude of the global outpouring of the Holy Spirit upon the world within the next five years.

Charles F. Parham, ironically was like the Apostle Peter in the Bible in the book of Acts dealing with the Gentile question concerning the infilling of the Holy Ghost. It states in Acts 10:11-15:

(11) And saw heaven opened, and a certain vessel descending upon him, as it had been a great sheet knit at the four corners, and let down to the earth: (12) Wherein were all manner of four-footed beasts of the earth, and wild beasts, and creeping things, and fowls of the air. (13) And there came a voice to him, Rise, Peter; kill, and eat. (14) But Peter said, not so, Lord; for I have never eaten any thing that is common or unclean. (15) And the voice spake unto him again the second time, what God hath cleansed, that call not thou common.

The Lord was showing Apostle Peter that he was about to take his ministry beyond his earthly prejudices, and that the Holy Ghost would fall upon all people and all races within the earth. The Lord knew that according to Jewish tradition he would not eat any rejected food, but God shows him unclean animals then ask him to eat it. Peter tells the Lord now you know I have never eaten anything unclean or common. The Lord answers Peter what God has cleansed, you have no right to call unclean.

Here God establishes the unclean food as an example of Gentiles who he would pour out his Spirit upon all flesh. In Peter's, experience the Jew thought the gospel was only for Jews, but God is the one who designates the spiritual boundaries of his predetermined movements within the earth.

Peter realizes that God's will and work is not bound by mankind's rules within this earth. It states in Acts 10:28, his full revelation about the limitation of race in the mind of God.

28. And he said unto them, Ye know how that it is an unlawful thing for a man that is a Jew to keep company, or come unto one of another nation; but God hath shewed me that I should not call any man common or unclean.

Peter reveals in this scripture God's method of seeing things that the racism of human beings doesn't limit the move of God on earth. This establishes in the New Testament God's view surrounding his sovereignty that any former teaching or views of prejudice do not limit him, and that he would pour out his Spirit upon all flesh.

As God established this principle in the New Testament church, by calling Paul to focus on the Gentiles because the other disciples allowed their prejudices to limit the spreading of the gospel to the utter most part of the earth. Sometimes God switches his choice of leaders depending upon their choices upon this earth.

The Bonnie Brae House where Bishop William Seymour held first prayer meeting in Los Angeles, California, 1906.

The question surrounding why Parham was not chosen to be the father of interracial worship and the globalization of Pentecostals was obvious. His own prejudice views excluded him from God's final choice.

Therefore, he is known as the founder of the beginning establishment of Pentecost in America, but God chose William J. Seymour to establish what Parham within his heart was not able to do.

In 1906, William J. Seymour relocated to Los Angeles, California to introduce his new teaching of speaking in tongues as the initial evidence of receiving the baptism of the Holy Spirit.

In September of 1906, Seymour admonishes Parham as his father in the gospel relating to his Pentecostal teaching. The Apostolic Faith paper that was published mentions William Seymour acknowledging Parham as the founder of modern day Pentecost. He requests that he come to see what God is doing in Los Angeles, California.

Los Angeles Times Newspaper Documenting People Speaking in Tongues at the Azusa Street Mission, 1906

Charles Parham comes to visit the Azusa Street Mission in October of 1906; six months after the Lord began to pour out his Spirit upon all races in the Los Angeles area.

The Apostolic News paper in 1906 reported that 150 people had received the experience of Pentecost in the Los Angeles area. These are some of the supernatural testimonies of God's working there in their midst.

1. People speaking in tongues
2. People with glasses healed not needing them
3. Man healed of asthma
4. God giving the gift of playing musical instruments
5. The gift of writing in unknown languages
6. Local churches receiving the Holy Ghost experience
7. Secular newspapers reporting these events
8. Man from the east speaks six language-received message in his language
9. People possessed with devils cast out
10. Girl of twelve years old receives the infilling
11. Young man healed of cancer

12. People giving thousand of dollar to send others to other nations with the Pentecostal message
13. Start the publishing of a paper that has testimonies of all occurrences at the Mission
14. Many have received the gift of songs in the Spirit
15. Nazarene brother receive the baptism of Holy Spirit
16. Reports of different individuals speaking different foreign languages, like Greek, Latin, Hebrew, French, German, Italian, Chinese, Japanese, Zulu
17. Daughter healed of consumption
18. Canes, crutches, medicine bottles, being thrown aside
19. Russian Churches hear their language spoken in their own tongues, and is converted to Pentecost
20. Many more testimonies too numerous to mention

      William J. Seymour tried to acknowledge Parham as his father in the gospel, but even with all the miracles, signs, and wonders Parham, upon his visit, allowed his racial prejudice to attack this God directed work.

The Azusa Street Mission Los Angeles, California

Upon Parham's arrival, Seymour graciously gave him the pulpit at the Azusa Street Mission. He openly expressed his disgust at the mix of whites with blacks, and the failure of blacks to recognize their "place." Parham later quoted himself:

I have seen meetings where all crowded around the alter, and laying across one another like hogs, blacks and whites mingling, this should be enough to bring a blush of shame to devils, let alone equals, and yet all this was charged to the Holy Spirit..."[13]

Parham allowed his bias views to attack the very glory of God. He split Seymour's church by asking whites to join him at another mission down the street.

William Seymour was shocked at Parham's reaction, but he never mentioned this in his paper wholly supporting Parham as a leader. He just stated that God was the true founder and projector of this movement.

This is why I believe that a year later Parham was arrested in San Antonio, Texas on sodomy charges. The word of God says," touch not my anointed and do my prophet no harm." The incident hurt Parham in the eyes of the Pentecostal Movement, and caused them to not recognize his place in the Pentecostal Movement.

Parham did not become recognized as the father of interracial worship and the globalization of Pentecostalism for obvious reasons. His own heart caused him to lose that mantle.

Even though Seymour was willing to hand it over to his predecessors without any reluctance on his part, God had seen fit to globalize it through Seymour's ministry. Nevertheless, God saw fit to set the boundaries on who would carry the torch of Pentecost to a global level. There was no room in the Inn in the heart of Parham to nurture what God had chosen to pour out.

Parham, like Peter's first reaction, rejected God's bringing all his children together to promote his kingdom business.

Chapter 3

The Azusa Street Revival wrapped in swaddling clothes, lying in a manger- St. Luke 2:12

In the words of Pastor William J. Seymour published in his January 1908 newspaper, states his spiritual view of the birth of Modern Day Pentecost:

"When Christ was born, it was in a barn at Bethlehem, and when He began sending the "latter rain" about two years ago, the outpouring of the Spirit; it was in a barn in Los Angeles, for the old Mission is like a barn in its humility and plainness. Its old beams and whitewashed walls have been ringing with the praises and songs of the children of God ever since. "[9]

The Apostolic Faith Newspaper Pastor William J. Seymour's monthly Publication 1906.

This brings me to the next chapter to outline what God's purpose and design was for one of the greatest moves of God in Modern Day history. In the book of Luke 2:7, it speaks of the birth of the Savior into the world. At the same time it illustrates something about God's reasoning and methodologies for the implementation of his plan. It says:

Luke 2 :(7) And she brought forth her firstborn son, and wrapped him in swaddling cloths and laid him in a manger; because there was no room for them in the inn. The word manger (Greek word phatne (fat-nay-a) means a place where animals eat, stall for animals). The Lord chose for the savior of the world to be born in a place where animals ate their food. It was in a beast of burdens stable where they lived that God desired the birth of his divine Son.

The Lord's choice was a rejected place. Not the place for a king to be born yet the angels and wise men came and pronounced him as such. This reminds me of the greatest birth of the Modern Day Pentecostal Movement. It was also born in a despised place the ghetto of Los Angeles, the black area of town.

Many had to come to a former Methodist Church that had been converted into an animal stable, where God's glorious fire spread throughout the world. The 1906 September issue of the Azusa Street newspaper had this quote by a white religious observer:

"Many churches have been praying for Pentecost, and Pentecost has come. The question is now will they accept it. God has answered in a way they did not look for. He came in a humble way as of old, born in a manger."[9]

The bible says the babe was wrapped in swaddling clothes. The meaning of swaddling clothes is a piece of the bottom of a base of the main garment.

Pastor William J. Seymour founder of the Azusa Street

William J. Seymour was born the son of ex-slaves. Could it be that God had selected him for such a time as this? As part of the humble piece of America's social fabric, he was not worthy based upon the racial views of American society.

Yet, God in all of his majesty as he did with his only begotten son Jesus, birth him in an environment unacceptable to our human views.

As the white observer stated, we prayed for Pentecost, and God has answered us. The Lord God decided to birth Modern Day Pentecost in swaddling cloths under the leadership of a son of ex-slaves.

This is not a question I believe of one race verses another, but God's way verses our way. As it states in the Bible Isaiah 55:8-9:

8. For my thoughts are not your thoughts, neither are your ways my ways, saith the LORD. 9. For as the heavens are higher than the earth, so are my ways higher than your ways, and my thoughts than your thoughts.

I believe it is an issue of God's sovereignty, which is a part of his attributes. He allows us to have our choices then he has his choices relating to whom he chooses. If we move away from him or do not accept his plan, we place ourselves in a position of making a choice other than his desire.

God has the right to choose another direction, or the right to choose a direction that he already knew we in our flesh would disagree with. He does this in order to get the glory out of the situation.

William J. Seymour always admired and acknowledged Charles Parham as the father of the modern day Pentecostal movement. Seymour writes in his news paper in October of 1906 surrounding Parham's covenant with God if the Lord would fill Charles Parham with the Holy Spirit, Parham quotes,

"The Lord said: " Are you able to stand for the experience in the face of persecution and howling mobs?" He said "Yes, Lord, if you will give me the experience, for the laborer must first be partaker of the firsts." Instantly the Lord took his vocal organs and he was preaching the Word in another language."[3]

The Lord's question to Parham in his own testimony was, are you able to stand for the experience in the face of persecution? Parham pledged to God he would only if he could receive the experience for himself.

Charles Parham, when he visited the Azusa Street Mission broke his covenant with God by coming against it by attacking the interracial worship of all God's children receiving the Holy Spirit without adhering to Jim Crow laws in America.

Mr. Charles Parham had to make a decision to accept what he did not understand, or be against this glorious move of God. Parham's racist views got the better of him, and he also realized that the persecution that would accompany this move of God would not defend it within his present society.

Ultimately, God will make choice of us but if we move away from his purpose he has the right to raise up a Paul that will take the gospel to the Gentiles. Those that are unacceptable, rejected, and despised by the "Status Quo" of our society, but embraced by a God of all the people.

Read I Corinthian 1:28, in the amplified version, which states,

> 28. And God also selected **(deliberately chose)** what in the world is low-born and insignificant and branded and treated with contempt, even the things that are noughting, that He might depose and bring to nothing the things that are.

The Lord chooses the foolish thing within America's society to confound the wise. He deliberately selected William J. Seymour and Bishop Charles Harrison Mason, who were the sons of ex-slaves that God anointed to be the swallowing cloths of the formative years of the Modern Day Pentecostal Movement.

It says in Corinthians that God selects the lowborn thing and things that are rejected by men. It was the same with Jesus being rejected by men, but being chosen by God. The Lord does this in order to proof to man that He is all-sovereign, and he will receive the glory out of a foolish looking situation.

This was the same way it was with Jesus being born in a rejected place, and the Azusa Street Revival being born in a rejected environment according to men's thinking. The Lord in all his glory allowed his only begotten son to be born in a horse stable, this would not have choice or the birthplace of the King of Kings.

Bishop William J. Seymour & Bishop Charles Harrison Mason

Also, it is the same with the Azusa Street Revival being born in the Ghetto's of Los Angeles, California, and at the same time two sons of ex-slaves became the most important figures in the formative years of the Pentecostal Movement.

The Lord's choice was to bring this movement right in the midst of an antagonistic political Jim Crow system within American society. His purpose was to birth forth a spiritual experience in America that would have a profound impact upon the history of American society.

When we become too saturated with traditions and religiousocity he will find someone's heart that is perfect before him. As it states in II Chronicles 16:9a:

For the eyes of the LORD run to and fro throughout the whole earth, to shew himself strong in the behalf of them whose heart is perfect toward him.

I believe the Azusa Street Revival was God's way of telling the world that all are his children, and God did not have to subject His move of the Spirit to the Jim Crow and segregation times his children lived in.

This was a statement from heaven down to earth that flesh and blood did not reveal it. The Pentecostals actually were given a gift from God that was to revolutionize Christendom and ultimately the mainline Protestant Movement.

The bases of Pastor William J. Seymour's theological doctrine was stated by himself in the September 1906 issues of his newspaper, which says,

We are not fighting men or churches, but seeking to displace dead forms and creeds and wild fanaticisms with living, practical Christianity." Love, Faith, Unity are our watchwords, and victory through the Atoning blood" our battle cry."[9]

Here is a quote from Bishop Ithiel C. Clemmon's book **Bishop C.H. Mason and the Roots of the Church of God in Christ** written in 1996 that supports this research surrounding the earlier interracial theological views of Seymour.

Seymour himself saw glossolalia as a sign but not as a proof of Spirit baptism, since the activity of the Spirit must also include evidence of love and communion between all nationalities. He stated in his first newspaper, "........multitudes have come. God makes no difference in nationality. Ethiopians, Chinese, Indians, Mexicans, and other nationalities worship together." 3

Pastor Seymour taught the original doctrinal view point that the sign of receiving the baptism is speaking in tongues, but the true manifestation is to display divine love to all God's children. If you look at the book of Acts 2:5, which states?

And there were dwelling at Jerusalem Jews, devout men, out of every nation under heaven. 6. Now when this was noised abroad, the multitude came together, and were confounded, because that every man heard them speak in his own language. 7. And they were all amazed and marveled, saying one to another, Behold, are not all these which speak Galileans? 8. and how hear we every man in our own tongue, wherein we were born?

Pastor William J. Seymour's Church Letterhead

William J. Seymour believed that the works of the Holy Spirit involved more than just displaying tongues, but his theological belief was that breaking down cultural barriers between races was the real manifestation of God's true kingdom truth.

This was the original doctrinal teaching of Seymour, and this is why he was the vessel of choice of God to introduce this to the whole world globally.

Also this establishes why Charles Parham was not chosen by God to enter this promise land, and it was his actions that caused him to only take the birthing of Modern Day Pentecost so far. He was chosen to establish and organize Modern Day Pentecost, but not to take it to its promise land to globalize it within the earth.

Obviously, racism was not apart of God's holy plan to reach all of his children because space, time or a certain group of people does not limit God. The bible explicitly states that heaven would be made up of all nations, kindred's, and tongues in Revelations 7:9, which reads:

> 9. *After this I beheld, and, lo, a great multitude, which no man could number, of all nations, and kindreds, and people, and tongues, stood before the throne, and before the Lamb, clothed with white robes, and palms in their hands.*

William J. Seymour's message was to transform his present society and prepare them for the coming Kingdom, and his soon coming King. He did not believe that the rules of our government took precedence over the true government of heaven.

The government of heaven included in Seymour's theological platform viewed a non-existent color line on earth as it is in heaven. He literally took God at his word that God's Kingdom was coming, and that His will being done on earth was to bring together the Body of Christ through the practice of true love for one another.

Bishop William J. Seymour Multicultural Congregation in 1906-09, Los Angeles, California

Basically, Seymour instituted with God's power behind him a vision that would literally transform America's Jim Crow society almost fifty years prior to the civil rights movement in America. The late Dr. Martin Luther King Jr., stated sixty years later, "The most segregated time in American is on Sunday morning when we all go to our several houses of worship based upon our color."

Dr. Martin Luther King Jr's., goal was to achieve desegregation through non-violent protest fifty years later. William J. Seymour experienced this utopia fifty years earlier. The over shadowing power of God's Spirit filled all races into one baptism and caused an immediate supernatural character change from racism to loving your neighbor as yourself. This is the second greatest commandment in the New Testament.

The theological position of William Seymour was the missing bases for Christianity, which was divorced of racial segregation, and embraced an interracial worship experience as God's spiritual civil rights activist.

The difference in the normal mainline denomination was that African Americans took their doctrine from their white counterparts. William Seymour and his protégé Bishop C.H. Mason developed their doctrinal position of interracial worship from God's revelation of them by the Holy Scriptures alone.

If Seymour had been the typical African American preacher during Jim Crow in America, he would have solicited his white father in the gospel's theological stance (Charles Parham) that God supported segregation of worship. Seymour ultimately rejected this and being a son of ex-slaves proclaimed a bold position that racism, sexism, and the like were wrong. The love of one another was necessary to bring the Body of Christ in alignment for her bridegroom and soon coming King.

How could we preach to the world the truth of God's love, but hypocritically stand on God's word as a justification of our own religious ideologies and political idiosyncrasies in American society. By this very revelation Seymour became one of the most influential African Americans in religious history, even with his short-lived sixteen years of Pentecostal ministry.

He felt that Pentecost brought all of God's children under one banner, and that if we were all truth the blood of Christ does wash away all of our sinful biases and indifferences. That these fleshly things can not withstand under God's power, if we truly embrace not just God's work only, but the God of the work.

Sometimes we as Christians spend so much time being busy serving God, but forget that in our first love we spend more time in the face of the master. This is how we conform to his very image by submitting to a life that includes prayer, fasting, and reading the word of God.

The foundation of Pentecost is seeking God's face through discipline prayer and fasting, seeking to be conformed by the power of the risen Christ.

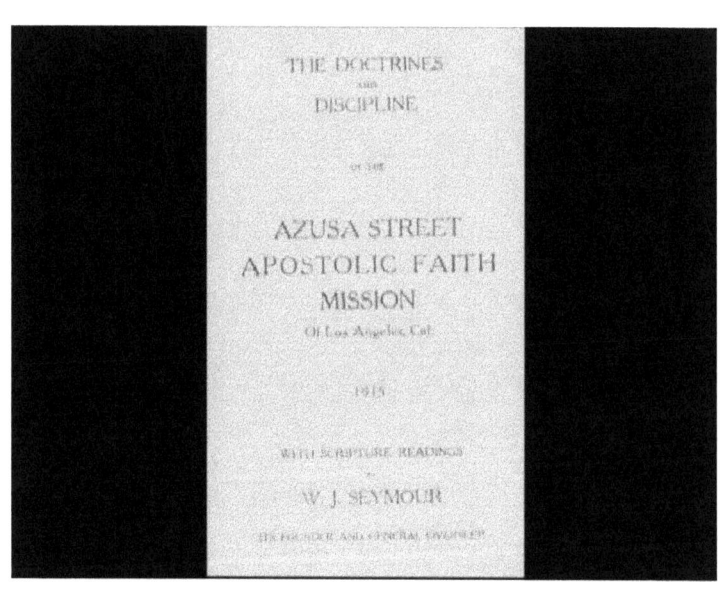

1915, Bishop William J. Seymour Publication that Documents the Doctrines of his Faith

Yet, today we have traded this experience with service with intimately laying before the God of the work, for example we do not mind being committed to church work or service, but not to consecrating and truly dedicating our life to God.

To know him truly is the antidote for the hypocrisy of mainstream religion misusing and abusing the Holy Scripture as grounds to uphold men's fleshly discriminating practices in America. Therefore, Seymour's theological view was in his day one of the most powerful expression of an African American churchman upon white Christianity. His influence and movement had a global impact upon Christendom.

William Seymour's central theological Pentecostal teaching and preaching of interracial unity, and the true manifested love of God through Holy living, was Seymour's central theme of his ministry. One thing that scholars left out of history was what was written on the side of the Azusa Street Mission.

Sign That Signified Pastor Seymour's Theme of This Ministry as Being Multicultural in 1906

It was Bishop William Seymour's ministry theme, which stated, "<u>Whosoever Shall Enter Here Let Brotherly Love Continue.</u>" The central focus of love being the true manifestation of the Holy Spirit's presence in the life of the believer was a necessity.

Seymour's theological genius given to him by God is one of the greatest revelations to Modern Christianity today. His belief yet at the same time is simple because God wants his spiritual family to live the word, by walking in divine love towards one another. Seymour, saw God's spiritual family being brought together again through biblically Holy Ghost inspired teaching that dispels biases as not having any biblical bases to stand on.

Chapter 4

Now I beseech you, brethren that there be no divisions among you   I Corinthians 1:10

Some may ask the question why you should be rehearsing the challenging events of the past. They are for our examples so that the Pentecostal Body of Christ understands that the spiritual challenges of their forefathers and mothers are the same challenges of today.

It is not God's will for divisions to exist within the Body of Christ. The bottom-line lesson surrounding these circumstances is to break down the barriers of racism, sexism, and differentiation of economic status within the Body of Christ.

I believe that God has, even with our own dysfunctions promoted us to the kingdom for such a time as this. That it is the Body of Christ's place to break down the walls of partition between denominations, races, genders, and nations, throughout the entire world.

Yet, three of the most deadly and damaging events occurred at the Azusa Street Mission and hindered the move of God. It did not stop it though, because God always has a ram in the bush, in order for his will to come to full maturity.

The first occurrence in the greatest Pentecostal move of God in America was the incident of Charles Parham's attack on interracial worship at the Azusa Street Mission, which split the church.

The bible says in I Corinthians 1: 10-13

10. Now I beseech you, brethren, by the name of our Lord Jesus Christ, that ye all speak the same thing, and that there be no divisions among you; but that ye be perfectly joined together in the same mind and in the same judgment. 11. For it hath been declared unto me of you, my brethren, by them, which are of the house of

Chloe, that there are contentions among you. 12. Now this I say, that every one of you saith, I am of Paul; and I of Apollos; and I of Cephas; and I of Christ. 13. Is Christ divided? was Paul crucified for you? or were ye baptized in the name of Paul?

The Apostle Paul witnessed this same spiritual battle of division in the Body of Christ, as a tool for Satan to be able to make our gospel less effective.

Charles Parham came to the Azusa Street Mission in October 1906, and attacked the move of God when he witnessed whites and blacks all worshipping together in the midst of God's manifested power.

The Spirit of God did not have to ask the permission or the view point of American society surrounding race and gender to establish this great out pouring of the Holy Ghost in America.

Neither governmental authorities, nor societal creeds and rules that limit certain races or people can bind the Holy Spirit.

The second issue of attack was the misunderstanding of Clara Lum. During most of Pastor William Seymour's ministry he had been a single man dedicating his life totally to the ministry.

Ms. Lum was a white sister who had assisted and worked closely with Seymour in the area of writing and maintaining the mailing list for Seymour's ministry. She desired to marry Pastor Seymour, and she fully believed that for whatever reason she was to be his wife.

Pastor Seymour was eventually feeling the pressure of the issue of deciding to get married, so in 1908 he wrote a letter to Bishop C.H. Mason to consult with another minister for Godly premarital counsel.

In 1948, Bishop Ithiel Clemmons interviews Bishop Mason surrounding what really occurred with

William Seymour and the Clara Lum controversy at the Azusa Street Mission, and Mason stated,

"According to Mason, Seymour told him that Clara Lum had privately made it clear that she fell in love with Seymour and wanted him to propose marriage to her. Seymour had tentatively considered the possibility and discussed the matter in its early stages with Mason who advised him not to even think about the idea." [4]

As a result Seymour decides to marry a black woman Ms. Jennie Evans Moore instead on May 13, 1908. The end result was Clara Lum's feelings being hurt. She left the Mission taking with her in revenge Pastor Seymour's mailing list and his Apostolic papers publication.

This controversy surrounding Seymour's marriage, and Clara Lum taking that part of Seymour's ministry ended the era of Seymour being able to connect with all his recipients globally.

Pastor Seymour Marries Jennie Instead of Clara Lum

At the Mission when Clara Lum left many other whites disagreed with Seymour's decision, and left his ministry also because they felt he should have married Ms. Lum.

There are actually three things that were established by the Holy Spirit at the Azusa Street Revival that mainline Christendom would have been uncomfortable with from their theological approaches.

The Holy Spirit with God's guidance chose to globalize Pentecost with three identifiable historical roots.

1. The diversity of races displaying interracial worship as part of the manifested presence of the evidence of glossolalia.

2. Selecting two sons of slaves, William J. Seymour & Bishop C.H. Mason as the most important figures in the earlier leadership of when God chose to introduce his

Modern Day Pentecostal movement to all nations, peoples, and tongues.

3. Selecting female leadership at the apex of the Azusa Street Revival to assist many future leaders in receiving the Baptism of the Holy Spirit.

These three things were obviously identifiable theological heritage of the earlier Twentieth Century Pentecostals. The Lord selected a way that would shock the more affluent mainline churches that detested the gender and racial harmony of the Azusa Street Revival.

Many faiths within mainline Christendom disagreed with what took place at the Mission. Their churches did not speak in tongues, have women in ministry, or conduct interracial worship. Neither was their leadership under a black man who was the son of ex-slaves.

This type of an environment was set in a time when people literally lynched blacks for participating in such activities. The physical and verbal persecution that came along with the founding forefathers and mothers of this earlier movement was not an easy task.

There were also white individuals that stood their ground in the Pentecostal Movement that refused to conform to bias towards other minority races. They remembered how their forefathers worshipped together with their African American brothers and sisters.

These individuals had to be committed to what they believe, and spiritual civil rights activist that came along with the "Outpouring" of the Holy Spirit persuaded them.

Obviously, they believed one of their tasks was spreading the gospel across all nations in order to move the world towards cultural reconciliation.

The goal was to spread the Pentecostal message to all nations, tongues, and people tearing down theological, gender, racial, and religious difference throughout the world.

Standing L-R, Adams, Boswell, Seated Pastor Seymour and John G. Lake their multicultural fellowship

From the time that the outpouring started hundreds of individuals sacrificed their lives to go into other nations of the world to spread the original Pentecostal messages. They believed that they were to bring the kingdom of God into place by all of God's creation under one faith.

Since Pastor Seymour's belief was that receiving the Holy Spirit equipped one to go to other nations and communities, many within four months immobilized local outreach and global missionary foreign field trips. Here is a statement from Seymour's newspaper October 1906, which confirms this:

Eight missionaries have started to the foreign field since this movement began in Los Angeles a few months ago. About thirty workers have gone out into the field. Missionaries for the foreign fields, equipped with several languages, are now on their way and others are only waiting for the way to open and for the Lord to say: "Go." We are on our faces before God. Let a volume of prayer go up from all the Lord's people. Awake! Awake!

There is but time to dress and be ready, for the cry will soon go forth. "The Bridegroom cometh."[9]

William Seymour's eschatological preaching positioned the Body of Christ to be prepared for the soon coming King. That there holiness demonstrated God's true love for all was their divine assignment in the earth.

His belief that the Kingdom of God was at hand, and that by spreading the Pentecostal message to the entire world was fulfilling the mandate of Jesus that stated, "Go ye into all the world, and preach the gospel to every creature."

Seymour's uncompromising gospel or his entire Pentecostal children still holds true today, that Pentecostals have the divine assignment to unify all people of all nations, people, and tongues in preparation of our Christ return to this earth.

Our heritage is yet before us to fulfill the lost doctrine of our founding father of Modern Day Pentecost. Even Pentecostals today have denied who they are by refusing to denounce biases they have embraced from mainline religion that is not the original teachings of William J. Seymour, their father in the gospel.

The question that still remains for Pentecostals globally is, will they take up the mantle of Seymour and return to their original commitment. This is to prepare all people to all nations to come together by receiving the Holy Ghost.

Also, Pentecostals should tear down the walls of race and gender partitions that divide the church of God today, and take up the battle cry to cleanse the body of her shortcomings. This will undoubtedly position her for preparation for effective ministry in these last days.

Chapter 5

Contending for the faith - Jude 1:3

The other individual who was the protégé of William J. Seymour, who was the son of ex-slaves, Bishop Charles Harrison Mason, and he was given the mantle of doctrine for the institution of Modern Day Pentecost. Bishop Mason was already a founder of a denomination in 1897 along with C.P. Jones ten years prior to the Azusa Street Revival that would take place in Los Angeles, California 1906.

He had evolved from the Baptist faith converting to the explosive Holiness doctrine that had been sweeping the southern United States. Bishop Mason and C.P Jones had been catapulted to fame in the Deep South by introducing the holiness doctrine to Baptist and Methodist through conventions, revivals, and periodicals.

Thousands of converts accepted Mason's uncompromising stand of living a Holy life before God. This shook the very foundation of the Baptist and Methodist faith, which caused many to desire to have more than just a religion.

They desired to know God for that involved a changed life of commitment from living any old way. Mason had established himself with God's divine favor as a denominational leader, and his organizational genius had built several churches. He had a large network of holiness churches under the Church of God in Christ banner between 1896-1899.

He came up with the name Church of God in Christ while walking along a road in Little Rock, Arkansas in 1897. Elder Mason, asked God to confirm his ministry which occurred by thousands souls being saved, many sick bodies being healed.

Yet, Mason, with all that God was doing in his life withdrew in prayer wanting to give up all that he had because it seemed like something was missing spiritually. He began to hunger and thirst after God in a greater way.

It was C.P. Jones, one of Mason's comrades and close friends who opened his eyes through the scriptures concerning the fact that they might have power to heal the sick, cast out devils, and yet not have the Holy Ghost infilling that took place on the Day of Pentecost (Acts 2:1, 2).

After they finished searching the scriptures C.P. Jones told Mason about the Day of Pentecost, and he stated that the same experience was the next level of their ministry. Mason states personally about brother C.P. Jones, "He opened Elder Mason's eyes to the fact that we did not have the baptism of the Holy Ghost according to Matthew 10:12, which showed clearly that we might have power to heal the sick, cast out devils and to raise the dead, and yet not have the baptism of the Holy Ghost with the evidence of speaking in tongues."

Bishop C.P. Jones the Chief Apostle of the Church of God in Christ Holiness

Ironically, that when Mason returns with the infilling five weeks later it is C.P. Jones who rejects Mason's glossolalia experience and forces Mason to start independently of his best friend, C.P. Jones, the Pentecostal side of the Church of God in Chris in Memphis, Tennessee in 1907.

In 1906, Mason had withdrawn in prayer before God. He heard about the Azusa Street's out pouring and two of his comrades went with him to spectator on this new Holy Ghost in filling experience, was this truly an actual move of God's Spirit in the earth?

He discovered that it was God's spiritual movement taking place at the Azusa Street Mission, and he humbled himself and desired to receive the Pentecostal experience for himself. His comrades were distracting him but what he was witnessing through Brother Seymour's ministry was real. The sick were healed; people spoke in another language and song in tongues.

His observations placed in him a hunger that was deeper than anything he had ever felt before. If the New Testament experience was real, then Mason wanted this Holy Ghost infilling for himself.

After the five week stay of the three ministers from Tennessee, it stated in Seymour's Apostolic Faith Periodical the date that C.H. Mason and his two minister friends had received the baptism of the Holy Spirit. This was recorded in the February-March issue, it stated,

*"March 19th was a wonderful day at the Mission on Azusa St. Three ministers from Tennessee received the endowment of power from on high and the glory of God filled the upper room. Others received the anointing of the Sprint, and some were slain under the power o God."*9

As Pastor Seymour was preaching all cultures worshipped together whites, blacks and Hispanics, and this Mason had not seen before this mixture of races within a black church. Mason had many dedicated white men in his ministry, but nothing like the multicultural worship he observed at the Azusa Street Mission.

When he attended the services at the mission he hungered for the empowerment that manifested in the New Testament Churches' evidence of speaking in tongues that was revealing itself under Seymour's ministry. The New Testament church of the book of Acts had come to life right before Mason's eyes, and he wanted all that God had in store for him before moving forward in his denominational structure and vision of the Church of God in Christ.

In Bishop C.H. Mason's personal testimony the first day arriving in Los Angeles in January of 1907, he stated,

"I began to thank God in my heart for all things for when I heard some speak in tongues I knew it was right, though I did not understand it."[6]

Mason was humbled by this experience of seeing God manifest his divine acts in the children of men. Mason took notice of the doctrinal teaching of Pastor William J. Seymour surrounding women in ministry, interracial worship, and divine love as the manifestation of the Holy Spirit Baptism.

These Azusa Street praying sisters assisted others receiving the wonderful experience of tongues as the initial evidence of the Holy Ghost infilling.

Mason gives a personal eyewitness account of the wonderful sermons and teachings of Elder Seymour while attending the services of the Azusa Street Mission. Elder Mason stated his personal observation of Elder Seymour's appeal and doxology that consisted of a three point appeal after the conclusion of his sermon, which stated,

"All of those that want to be sanctified or baptized with the Holy Ghost, go to the upper room, and those that

want to be healed go to the prayer room, and those that want to be justified, come to the alter."[6]

Mason stated that his words were sweet and powerful; it seems that I can still hear his words while I am writing this statement. Mason tells of his experience of meeting Elder Seymour upon his first visit at the Azusa Street Mission, He states,

"Just as I attempted to bow down someone called me and said, the pastor wants you three brethren in his room, I obeyed and went up."[6]

He received us and seemed to be so glad to see us there. Pastor William Seymour stated,

"Brethren, the Lord will do great things for us and bless us. He cautioned us not to be running around in the city seeking worldly pleasure, but seek pleasure of the Lord."[6]

Bishop Charles Harrison Mason

The second night of service at the Azusa Street Mission Bishop C.H. Mason saw a vision as God's presence filled the room. He stated,

"I saw myself standing alone and had a dry roll of paper. I had to chew it. When I had gotten it all in my mouth trying to swallow it, looking up towards the heavens there appeared a man at my side. I turned my eyes at once, then I awoke and the interpretation came. God had me swallowing the whole book, and that if I did not turn my eyes to anyone but God and Him only, He would baptize me." [6]

This vision that Mason saw revealed to him how he would carry the Pentecostal doctrine of Seymour as a part of his message to the world through his Church of God in Christ organization he had started ten years earlier.

Later this vision becomes true because Mason becomes one of the most influential leaders in the infancy stage of the Modern Day Pentecostal Movement.

To also confirm this point, almost twelve years later the tables would turn, and William J. Seymour would be visiting Bishop C.H. Mason at his world headquarters during his 12th Holy Convocation in Memphis, Tennessee in December of 1919.

This event occurred three years before William Seymour died in March of 1922. This special visit that he made was to acknowledge, and place his blessing upon the importance of the Church of God in Christ movement within the future of Modern Day Pentecost.

This paragraph was recorded by recording secretary in the assembly of hundred or more pastors and overseer throughout the United States that followed the ministry of Chief Apostle Bishop Charles Harrison Mason. The minutes stated in December 10, 1919 Thursday morning three years before the death of Pastor Seymour, secretary writes in the minutes,

"Elder W.J. Seymour of Chicago, who also was one of the founders of this great movement, came to us at this

hour. How glad our hearts were made to meet him. Order of business was suspended for a few minutes to greet him. Elder Seymour then spoke of his long and wearisome trip and how glad he was to get here. He said he looked upon the Church of God in Christ to be the greatest movement on earth. Therefore he rejoiced to stand among the greatest people on earth. He asked us to contend for the doctrine. He also repudiated even the thought of fornication in the ministry. In his conclusion he urged that the ministry not only be fruitful but to show their fruits. Chief Apostle Mason made some very timely remarks by way of responding in the noble sayings of Elder Seymour. He concluded by singing in the spirit a song of welcome." 8

Here, ironically, Mason sits under the ministry of Seymour at the Azusa Street Mission for five weeks as a denominational leader. It is twelve years later three years prior to Seymour's death he personally profess and prophesy before a full house then gives Bishop Mason his blessing that God has allowed him to raise up one of the greatest groups that the Pentecostal world will see.

The Azusa Street Mission where Bishop C.H. Mason received the Baptism of the Holy Ghost in March of 1907

Elder Mason is at the Azusa Street Mission, while seeking God for the Pentecostal experience. The Lord gives him a vision of a man standing next to him asking him to eat the entire roll. Is God going to give him the baptism of the Holy Spirit?

Elder Mason acknowledges the heavenly vision to carry the essence of the original doctrine of Pentecost that he delivered to Pastor William J. Seymour. Bishop Mason did not know the magnitude of his spiritual destiny, at the Azusa Street Mission in February 1907.

Bishop C.H. Mason begins to seek God for the baptism of the Holy Ghost with all of his heart even more, then He stated,

"Then one of the praying sisters came over to Elder Mason she told him that the devil will try to make you feel sad, but this is not the way to receive Him you must be glad and praise the Lord. He observed another sister that prayed for another brother prophesying to him, and he fell on his knees before her to receiving prayer to

*receive the baptism with evidence of speaking in tongues."*₆

Bishop Mason stood right next to them while the gentleman received the evidence of speaking in tongues. It made Elder Mason want to fall to his knees. He desired it so bad for himself he did not know what to do. Bishop C.H. Mason reveals his eye wittiness accounts and his personal testimony of how he sought God for the Holy Ghost, he stated,

"Then I began to seek for the baptism of the Holy Ghost according to Act 2:44, which readeth thus: "Then they that gladly received His word were baptized."
Then I saw that I had a right to be glad and not sad. As the enemy was trying to make me believe the way to receive the Holy Ghost was to be sad, but the light of the word put him out. There came a reason in my mind which said, Were you sad when you were going to marry? I said, No, I was glad." It said that this meant wedlock to Christ. Then I saw more in being glad than in being sad."

Florence Crawford one of the woman that assisted in praying with other to receive the Baptism of the Holy Ghost in 1907.

One of the Azusa Street praying sisters was active in assisting individuals in praying through to the Holy Ghost. Mason was assisted with Acts 2:44, which she shared with him while working with him to receive the baptism experience. This information helped him to understand that he needed to rejoice if he was to receive this experience for himself.

The music of the Azusa Street Revival was jubilantly rejoicing. Mason leads the saints in a song during praise service, He stated:

"Then I began to seek for the baptism of the Holy Ghost according to Act 2:44, which readeth thus: "Then they that gladly received His word were baptized."
Then I saw that I had a right to be glad and not sad. As the enemy was trying to make me believe the way to receive the Holy Ghost was to be sad, but the light of the word put him out. There came a reason in my mind which said, Were you sad when you were going to marry? I said, No, I was glad." It said that this meant wedlock

to Christ. Then I saw more in being glad than in being sad."6

One o the Azusa Street praying sisters was active in assisting individuals in praying through to the Holy Ghost. Mason was assisted with Acts 2:44, which she shared with him while working with him to receive the baptism experience. This information helped him to understand that he needed to rejoice if he was to receive this experience or himself.5

Here is Mason's actual testimony of receiving the infilling of the Holy Spirit at Azusa Street Mission. He testified of his personal experience as a denominational leader about receiving the infilling of the Holy Ghost.

The music of the Azusa Street Revival was jubilantly rejoicing. Mason leads the saints in a song during praise service, He stated;

"Some said let us sing. I arose and the first song that came to me was, "He brought me out of the miry clay, He sat my feet on the Rock to stay." The Spirit came

upon the saints and upon me. I soon sat down and soon my hands went up and I resolved in my heart not to take them down until the Lord Baptized me."[6]

"The sound of a mighty wind was in me and my soul cried, Jesus, only, none like you. My soul cried and soon I began to die. It seemed that I heard the groaning of Christ on the cross dying for me. All of the work in me until I died out of the old man. The sound stopped for a little while. My soul cried, Oh, God finish your work in me. Then the sound broke out in me again. Then I felt something raising me out of my seat without any effort of my own. I said, It may be my imagination. I saw that I was rising. Then I gave up, for the Lord to have His way in me. So there came a wave of glory into me, and all of my being was filled with the glory of the Lord. Therefore, when He had gotten me straight on my feet there came a light, which enveloped my entire being above the brightness of the Sun. When I opened my mouth to say glory, a flame touched my tongue, which ran down in me. My language changed and no word could I speak in my own tongue."[6]

This experience of Bishop C. H. Mason receiving the baptism of the Holy Spirit under William J. Seymour's ministry at the Azusa Street Revival took place on March 19, 1907.

In the November 28, 1908 one year later, Bishop C.H. Mason writes the Apostolic Faith Publication sharing his testimony about his battle with C. P. Jones who expelled him because of his experience of being filled with the Holy Ghost at the Azusa Street Revival. Here is some of his dialogue, which states,

"Dear ones, it is sweet for me to think of you and your kindness to me while I was with you. My soul is filled with the glory of the Lord. He is giving great victory wherever He sends us in His name, many being baptized with the Holy Ghost and speaking in tongues. Praise the Lord. The fight has been great. I was put out, because I believed that God did baptize me with the Holy Ghost among you all. Well, He did it and it just suits me. Glory in the Lord. Jesus is coming. Take the Bible way, it is right. The Lord is leading me out of all

that men have fixed up for their glory. Be strong in Him. (Isa. 41:10, 20). The Lord is casting out devils, healing the sick, and singing the sweetest songs. I do not have time to go back over one to practice it, for the next will be new. Praise His name. I sit under His shadow with great delight, His banner over me is love."[9]

Bishop Mason's belief in the principle of Devine love that Seymour taught encouraged him to look at C. P. Jones as his brother despite his rejection of himself. The real bible evidence of their daily walk had to do with them practicing what they preached. The tongues not the only sign of the out pouring of the Holy Spirit, many wanted to be preoccupied with the gift and not the fruit of the Holy Spirit.

When it came to loving their brother or sister to the point of not participating in lynching or Jim Crow practices as a Christian way of life. Seymour and Mason taught that if you truly had the Holy Ghost of the New Testament you would not participate in racial practices.

In the book of Acts Chapter 2:1-14, Seymour and Mason taught that tongues without the signs of reaching out to break down barriers of other cultures was an ineffective Christianity. When they spoke in tongues they were able to unify those that were divided by race and language barriers, in order to extend the gospel message to other people, nations, and tongues.

The Seymour-Mason theological perspectives took on an eschatological message that for God's bride to be ready she must be cleaned from all these fleshly man made bias conception of America's culture. That the Pentecostal's were carving out a message of reconciliation of all God's children, in order for the true government of heaven or Kingdom of heaven to materialize on this earth before Christ return.

The church of God had a mandate to truly live God's word, and not to take on the hypocrisy of mainline Christianity that fostered malice, hatred, and prejudice hidden and justified behind the word of God. This was the true unadulterated doctrinal teaching of the Azusa Street Mission, which was God's secret and God's divine plan, that is the spiritual legacy of Pentecostalism in America,

Bishop Charles Harrison Mason became the Paul who came along later after men like Parham and Seymour, but God used them to become the protégés and doctrinal leaders of the earlier years of Modern Day Pentecost in America.

Mason left his Azusa experience but refused to be denied the opportunity to contend for the faith that was once delivered to the saints at the Azusa Street Mission. Holding firm to the scripture in Jude 1:3, which states:

"Beloved, when I gave all diligence to write unto you of the common salvation, it was needful for me to write unto you, and exhort you that ye should earnestly contend for the faith which was once delivered unto the saints,"

Mason's heart was not just to uphold the relevance of the importance of speaking in tongues as the initial evidence, but supporting divine love too redefines the religious and political ideologies of mainstream Christian. That the Holy Spirit baptism was a means to an end to unite all of God's people on the earth as a color-blind and non-racial family in the earth was God's true desire for his kingdom family in the earth.

One of Mason's famous says from the scriptures that penetrated his denominational culture was found in Hebrews 12:14, it states, *"Follow peace with all men, and holiness without no man shall see the Lord."*

The holiness theme from the older saints was that you had to live right in order or your testimony to have any real substance. This included true holiness meant to pursue peace with all men, for instance, you in Mason's view could not profess the Holy Ghost and be at odds with your brother.

Bishop Charles Harrison Mason

How can one stand on the integrity of God's word, and desire to harm one's sister or brother because of racism? In Mason theological worldview one needed to go back to the altar to truly receive the Holy Ghost because the gift came with the fruits of the Spirit. His believe was no man shall see the Lord without this type of true integrity of treating one another right.

Bishop C.H. Mason ministry had a low tolerance for individuals who just wanted to have religiousocity. He encouraged them to live what they preached by loving their brother and to follow peace with all men. Many of the strict biblical standards of Mason's denominational tradition would be a cultural shock to modern day Christianity today.

Bishop C.H. Mason, took Seymour's non-racial theological platform of divine love, and broadens and institutionalized that prospective within the modern day Pentecostal Movement.

Bishop Seymour's Doctrinal Handbook in 1915

The impact of Bishop Mason's profound organizational genius during the infancy stage of Modern Day Pentecost became one of the most direct influences upon black churchmen in Modern Day Christendom.

Here are some of the many ways that Mason's influence took interracial relationship to the next level with Pentecostalism in America.

1. From 1909-14 Mason institutionalized interracial and nonracist interaction by allowing white Pentecostal to administratively carry his credentials.
2. In 1916-1919 Mason conducted healing campaigns in city auditoriums for all white groups, therefore institutionalizing interracial worship at a time when segregation practices was the culture of American history.
3. In 1914, in Hot Springs, Arkansas Mason was invited to speak and attended the first Assembly of God convention, where he was looked to by white Pentecostals to invoke his blessing upon the start of their denomination.

4. In 1907, institutionalized interracial and nonracial interaction by appointing a white brother to a national position William B. Holt as his national recording secretary.

5. In 1918, Mason institutionalized interracial and nonracial interaction by submitting a pacifist and conscious objector stance with US Government, which cause thousands white and black Pentecostal to unify surrounding the draft laws surrounding WWI.

6. In 1918-1919, Mason institutionalized interracial and nonracial positioning that provoked the FBI and the United States government prosecute Mason for treason against the United States government.

7. In 1911, Mason appointing a women to a national position within his denomination, keeping with Seymour's visibility of women working along side the men in ministry.

Bishop C.H. Mason demonstrated the true essence of the first-century apostle's mantle, and was the greatest example of an Apostle in the twentieth-century Pentecostal movement that personally received the baptism of the Holy Spirit at the Azusa Street Mission in 1907. His adamant desire to maintain the true essence of the Azusa Street Revival allowed the type of growth that led to his organization becoming one of the largest African American Pentecostal organizations in American history.

Chapter 6
Conclusion Saint John 17:11

Pentecostal's divine assignment in the Last days break down the walls of division spiritually and economically. The last prayer of Jesus towards the Body of Christ was that they might be one. It states this in St. John 17:11;

11. And now I am no more in the world, but these are in the world, and I come to thee. Holy Father, keep through thine own name those whom thou hast given me, that they may be one, as we are.

I believe that Christ saw through time that the greatest fight the church would have is division amongst themselves. This is why he hopes that we might be one.

The present day Body of Christ is divided into different faiths or denominations.

I believe that the forefathers of the Pentecostal movement have been given the gift originally of interracial worship, and the power to tear down the barriers of differences between races and people. They have been given the gift of the Holy Spirit Baptism in these last days to bring together the Body of Christ as never before.

This is why the Azusa Street Centennial Celebration is so important in the spiritual realm; it symbolizes Pentecostalism embracing its roots.

Within its roots abide the faith, hope, and charity that the concept Christendom needs to come together as one. For the bride of Christ is to be prepared to show the unity that will cause them to be ready to meet the world's needs in the end?

The Holy Spirit infilling brings individuals together whether they are in another denomination or not. The original divine love doctrine is the answer to bring commonality to the entire Body of Christ.

I believe that we have to come to the kingdom for such a time as this, but we need to mature in the area of being more sensitive to the multitude.

The leaders of the Pentecostal Movement have prospered greatly. If we do not come into full spiritual maturity we will think that our individual prosperity is our true purpose. Our true purpose is not to build up bigger barns in ministry financially, but to be as Joseph's in the end and realize God placed us where we are for others' posterity, not just our own.

As it states in Genesis (3) And Joseph said unto his brethren, I am Joseph; doth my father yet live? And his brethren could not answer him; for they were troubled at his presence. (4) And Joseph said unto his brethren, Come near to me, I pray you. And they came near. And he said, I am Joseph your brother, whom ye sold into Egypt. (5) _Now therefore be not grieved, nor angry with yourselves, that ye sold me hither: for God did send me before you to preserve life_. (6) For these two years hath the famine been in the land: and yet there are five years, in which there shall neither be earning nor harvest. (7) _And God sent me before you to preserve you a posterity in the earth, and to save your lives by a great deliverance._ (8) So now it was not you that sent me hither, but God: and he hath made me a father to Pharaoh, and lord of his entire house, and a ruler throughout all the land of Egypt.

The forefathers and mothers of the Pentecostal Movement suffered much reproach to bear in their bodies the testimony of Jesus and the testimony of glossolalia in modern Day Pentecost. Now God has prospered those of the Pentecostal faith in America the rejected faith in the past by mainstream religion. Unlike Joseph who was rejected by his brethren, God has prospered the Pentecostal faith.

He has promoted and prospered us among our brethren of the mainline religion. In the area of grow of our churches, globally known spiritual leaders, and control of Christian media outlets.

The seeds of William J. Seymour's ministry in 1906 have come to the forefront as those in whom God will place the burden of providing strategic plan of wealth transference for Christendom as a whole.

There is a period of time coming upon the earth as in Joseph's day where the money shall fail, but before that God will allow the wealth of the world be laid up for the righteous. The Lord has not just brought us to the kingdom for such a time as this to prosper individually, but to come to full maturity and realize that where you are is not just for yourself but for others.

It says in the book of Esther 4:13-14:

13. Then Mordecai commanded to answer Esther, Think not with thyself that thou shalt escape in the king's house, more than all the Jews. 14. For if thou altogether holdest thy peace at this time, then shall there enlargement and deliverance arise to the Jews from another place; but thou and thy father's house shall be destroyed: and who knoweth whether thou art come to the kingdom for such a time as this?

Mordecai reminded Esther that she was in a place or season greater than herself and her own house. Many leaders in the Pentecostal Movement have been put into place for such a time as this.

Not just to preach the gospel of the kingdom, but to unmask the wealth of God's kingdom to help the multitude when the time great lack will come.

The kingdom of God will be rich with substances, not just individual's wealth, but those Joseph's will come to provide a system financially that can not be broken even during troubled economic times in the world. There will come a time when there will be a spirit of unity like has never existed before amongst Pentecostals.

The 100th Year Azusa Street Centennial Celebration in 2006 is the first time all of our denominational streams had come together.

The Lord Jesus prayed that they might be one, and that the creatures waited in expectation of the sons of God, for us to demonstrate the fact that God's human family is multicultural. The time will come that we will build up barns of wealth, but not just for ourselves individually, but God will bring out Joseph's in the Body of Christ that will unmask the wealth o God's kingdom or all not just for a few.

This will be to prepare the way of the Lord's kingdom in the earth that the world will have to come to the Pentecostal Movement for its help. As Joseph was needed to use the gifts of divine insight in order to bring deliverance upon the earth.

Right now we are not looking to the future, and we are waiting for the world to know what God will give to us spiritually. We are placing our trust in governments instead of realizing that we are the true government in the earth until Christ returns.

The Lord Jesus told us how to pray that God's kingdom will come, and that his will be done in earth as it is in heaven. His will is that his bride unifies, so that they will become more preparatory as if they know the future.

The Pentecostal Body of Christ needs to allow their prophetic eyes to see ahead, so that as Joseph we will know what Pharaoh could not know. We will be able to see how to prepare a kingdom of resources that the world will have to come to for help.

The issue of buying and selling was changed during Joseph's time of famine. It says in the Bible that the value of their dollar had diminished to nothing. As it states in Genesis 47:15, which says:

15. And when money failed in the land of Egypt, and in the land of Canaan, all the Egyptians came unto Joseph, and said, Give us bread: for why should we die in thy presence? for the money faileth.

This is symbolic of the times close to the end when the economic positioning of the world will be at a strain. The money of the world will be at a strain, but the spiritual wealth and resources of the unified Pentecostal Body of Christ will not.

Even before this time God will organize and galvanize his Joseph's in the Pentecostal Body of Christ to begin to build up the wealth of God's kingdom in the earth. Many will not want to do it because their hearts are towards only themselves, and they will not be mature enough to see that they are in position within the kingdom or others and not just themselves.

As it states in Revelations 13:17, which states:

" And that no man might buy or sell, save he that had the mark, or the name of the beast, or the number of his name."

In the economy, the issue of buying and selling will be controlled by the world system. It is not the will of God for the church to be subject to the world. Before this time there will be a great harvest of wealth for the church, in order to provide for God's people prior to the great tribulation.

The signs of the times are the break down in the economy. The Lord told us to occupy until I come. We have work to do in order to prepare for the coming of God's kingdom.

WORKS CITED

1. James Delk, He Made Millions Happy (Hopkinsville, KY:Privately Published, 1950).

2. Douglas J. Nelson, "For Such a Time as This: The Story of Bishop William J. Seymour and the Azusa Street Revival, a search for Pentecostal/Charismatic Roots," (Ph.D. diss, University of Birmingham, England, May 1981), 196-199.

3. Sherry Sherrod DuPree, "Biographical Dictionary of African American, Holiness-Pentecostals", Publisher: Middle Atlantic Regional Press, Washington, D.C., 1989.

4. Bishop Ithiel C. Clemmons, "Bishop C.H. Mason and the roots of the Church of God in Christ," Publisher: Pneuma Life Publishing, Bakersfield, Califoria, 93389.

5. Elijah L. Hill, Women Come Alive, Arlington, Texas, P.O. Box 181937, (Independently Published www.ptkim.org), May, 2005

6. James Courts, "The History and Life Work of Bishop C.H. Mason", Privately Published: Memphis, TN, 1919.

7. David A. Hall, Sr, Essays to the Next Generation", Independently Published: Memphis, TN, 2004.

8. Minutes of the 12th Annual Holy Convocation, Church of God in Christ, Memphis, TN (November 1919), p. 13-14. Files of Geraldine Wright, Southfield, Michigan.

9. William J. Seymour Editor, "The Apostol Faith Newsletters" Vol. 1-Vol II No. 13, September 1906-1908, Republisher by The Apostolic Faith Gospel Mission 1906-1909.

10. Frank Bartleman, "Azusa Street", Publisher, Logos International, Plainfield, NJ 07060, 1980.

11. Gayraud Wilmore, "The Black Church and Black Radicalism", Publisher: Maryknoll, NY:Orbis Books, 1983.

12. Charles H. Pleas, "Fifty Years of Achievement:Church of God in Christ, Privately Published: Kansas City, KS, 1955.

13. Vinson Synan, "The Holiness-Pentecostal Movement in the U.S., Publisher: William B. Erdmans, Grand Rapids, MI, 1971.

14. Cheryl Townsend-Gilkes, "Power Among the Powerless: The Santified Church' and the Reorganization of Black Religion," paper presented at the Society for the Scientific Study of Religion, October 22, 1982.

15. James S. Tinney, "Black Origins of the Pentecostal Movement," Christianity Today, 16, no. 1, October 1971.

16. James S. Tinney and Stephen N. Short, Eds. "In the Tradition of William J. Seymour, Publisher: Spirit Press, Washington, D.C., p. 15-16,1978.

17. Morris E. Golder, "History of the Pentecostal Assemblies of the World, Indianapolis, Indiana, p. 17-20, 1973.

18. Cornel West, "Prophesy Deliverance," Published by Westminister Press, p. 69-91, 1982.

19. Sydney Ahlstrom, "The Religious History of the American People, Published by:Yale University Press, New Haven, CT, p.1063, 1972.

20. David D. Daniels, "God Makes no Differences in Nationality:The Fashioning of a New Racial/Nonracial Identity at the Azusa Street Revival," in Enrichment

Journal, ed Gary R. Allen and Rich Knoth, (Springfield, Missouri) Issue Spring 2006, Vol. 11, No. 1, Pg. 72-76.

21. Jon Michael Spencer, "Protest and Praise:Sacred Music of Religion, Published by Fortress Press, 1990.

22. William C. Turner, "The United Holy Church:A Study in Black-Holiness Pentecostalism," (Ph.D. diss. Duke University, 1984.

23. Leonard Lovett, "Black-Holiness Pentecostalism:Inplications for Ethnics and Social Transformation," (Ph.D. diss. Emory University, Candler School of Theology, 1979).

24. Burgess, Stanley M., and McGee, Gary B., "Dictionary of Pentecostal and Chrismatic Movements, Published by Zondervans, Grand Rapids, MI, 1988.

25. William J. Seymour, "Doctrines and Disciples of the Azusa Street Apostolic Faith Mission of Los Angeles, Privately Published: Los Angeles, CA, 1915.

26. Cheryl Townsend-Gilkes, "Cultural Constituencies in Conflict:Religion, Community, Reorganization and Rise of the Saints, 1890-1925," Association of Black Sociologists and the Society for the Study of Social Problems, 1983.

27. Leonard Lovett, "Aspects of the Spiritual Legacy of the Church of God in Christ:Ecumenical Implications," Published by Midstream 24, April 1985, p. 389-397

28. The Federal Bureau of Investigation, "Investigative files and records on Bishop Charles Harrison Mason because of his pacifism and interracialism," Documented in:Washington, D.C., 1918.

29. A. M. Cotton, "Inside Story of the Outpouring of the Holy Spirit, Azusa Street, April 1906." Message of the "Apostolic Faith" 1, 1939, p. 1-3.

30. Cecil M. Robeck, Jr., "Azusa Street Revival, " in Dictionary of Pentecostal and Charismatic Movements,

ed. Stanley M. Burgess and Gary B. McGee (Grand Rapids: Zondervan, 1988, 33.

31. Ithiel C. Clemmons, "Charles Harrison Mason," in Dictionary of Pentecostal and Charismatic Movements, ed. Stanley M. Burgess and Gary B. McGee (Grand Rapids: Zondervan, 1988, 585-588.